THE REAL YOU

MANIFESTING KINGDOM IDENTITY

ACTIVATION MANUAL

LINDA BREITMAN

Published by Linda Breitman Ministries.
© 2013 by Linda Breitman

Unless otherwise indicated, all Scripture quotations are from:

The Holy Bible, New International Version®, NIV®.
Copyright © 1973, 1978, 1984, 2011 by Biblica, Inc.™ Used by permission of Zondervan. All rights reserved worldwide. The "NIV" and "New International Version" are trademarks registered in the United States Patent and Trademark Office by Biblica, Inc.™

Additional Scripture quotations:

Scripture quotations marked (AMP) are taken from the Amplified Bible, Copyright © 1954, 1958, 1962, 1964, 1965, 1987 by The Lockman Foundation. Used by permission.

Scripture quotations marked (NASB) are taken from the New American Standard Bible®, Copyright © 1960, 1962, 1963, 1968, 1971, 1972, 1973, 1975, 1977, 1995 by The Lockman Foundation Used by permission.

Scripture quotations marked (NKJV) are taken from the New King James Version®. Copyright © 1982 by Thomas Nelson, Inc. Used by permission. All rights reserved.

Scripture quotations marked (ESV) are taken from The Holy Bible, English Standard Version, which is adapted from the Revised Standard Version of the Bible, copyright Division of Christian Education of the National Council of the Churches of Christ in the U.S.A. All rights reserved.

Printed in the United States of America
ISBN-10: 0989411311
ISBN-13: 978-0-9894113-1-8

For information contact:
Linda Breitman Ministries
LindaBreitman.com

I DEDICATE THIS BOOK TO MY BELOVED MOTHER WHO ALWAYS BELIEVED IN ME.

I ALSO DEDICATE THIS BOOK TO MY WONDERFUL HUSBAND—KING TURKEY—WHO CONSTANTLY HAS MY BACK SPIRITUALLY AND GRAMMATICALLY! I LOVE YOU! QUACK!

ACKNOWLEDGMENTS

I would like to acknowledge Lauren Gallaway for overseeing the entire *Real You* project. Your great ideas and hard work have been invaluable. You've overcome so many challenges and are always positive. You carry not only the favor of God but also the joy of the Lord. We have been on an exciting journey together—with each day bringing more fun. So many days I've felt like we have gone where no man has been before! Yay!

I am grateful for all the hours my dear husband Les invested in editing. You are brilliant. You make me look good! Quack!

Joanne Stroud, thank you for your on-going intercession for this project. You have persevered with me for the past few years and helped me finally deliver this baby. I am deeply grateful for how you continually imparted wisdom and encouragement.

Debra Hogervorst is a gifted director, producer, cinematographer, and editor. I appreciate your creativity and dedication. The teaching videos came out great—very down-to-earth and authentic. I so appreciate our friendship.

Thanks to Kat Flippin for extensive research, proofreading, and handling so many details. You are a joy.

Thanks to all those who prayed, encouraged and supported me in some way—John and Judy Ross, Nate Firth, Steven Anderson, Jim and Julia Pinzenscham, Tom McGurin, Mike Hubbard, Annette Moreno, Aaron Jayne, Bob Cathers, and Bill Yount. I would like to thank the girls, my beautiful spiritual daughters. You have been an inspiration to me. All our years together have more fully formed the revelation on identity. There are so many more I would like to thank. I have been blessed with so many amazing friends. Thank you all.

Endorsements

Change doesn't begin around you until it is identified within you. Your mind is the birthplace for your feelings, your function, and your future realities. In this magnificent book, Linda Breitman has opened the door for unlimited miracles to fill your life as you begin to understand your new identity in Christ. Step-by-step you will journey into a profound comprehension of God's overwhelmingly good thoughts toward you. Once you have saturated in the wealth of revelation found within the pages of this gem, you will unmistakingly know that you are accepted, valued, and chosen by God. This book will help to bring a paradigm shift into your mind... that will overflow into your life. Get ready to receive the change that you've prayed for... read this book and you will be blessed!

JOSHUA MILLS
International Conference Speaker and Best-selling Author
31 Days To A Miracle Mindset
Vancouver, BC, Canada
www.JoshuaMills.com

Linda's book helps us to listen to the correct inner tapes of who we really are and what God's destiny is for us. You will never feel comfortable in your own skin until you realize how God has made you, your giftings, your passion, your design. This book is critical to that process. Read it, walk through it, and watch as your identity crisis gets unpeeled and unwrapped and the real you stands up.

GARY GOODELL
Third Day Churches, Inc.
Author of, *Permission Granted To Do Church Differently in the 21st Century,* and *Where Would Jesus Lead?*

As blood-bought, Spirit-filled believers, we have a mandate to release the Kingdom of Heaven into the earthly realm—loosing miracles, prosperity, restoration of families, and the very blueprints of heaven. We are the "doors" and "gates" of the supernatural—the very conduits through whom heaven touches earth. For some, however, after the born again experience occurs, these pathways and mental faculties never fully open to the reality of the supernatural that comes from the renewal of the mind and living from our new heavenly identity. In her book, Linda Breitman releases not only the truth of your new nature in Christ but provides high level activation exercises to renew your mind according to the Word of God, allowing the supernatural to flow as you begin living as the real you. Read it. Apply it. Live it.

JEFF JANSEN
Founder, Global Fire Ministries International
Global Fire Church & World Miracle Center
Kingdom Life Institute
Author, *Glory Rising* and *Furious Sound of Glory*
www.globalfireministries.com

These are days of consummation, fullness, and harvest. Clearly all seeds sown into the earth are coming to maturity simultaneously. The sons of the Kingdom must respond to this call by understanding who they are in Christ and the potential He imparts to us. As we learn to posture ourselves in perfect alignment with heaven, the flow of the Lord's nature and ability will find its resting place in us. Linda Breitman has captured the essence of that mandate and provided incredible tools to help us fulfill our destiny and purpose. The biblical truths and practical applications you'll discover in this book will prove invaluable in your pursuit of the Lord and personal destiny. It is for that purpose that I recommend *The Real You: Believing Your True Identity* to any believer hungry for God and the fullness of His purposes.

PAUL KEITH DAVIS
WhiteDove Ministries

Linda Breitman is a friend, leader, and mentor of many. She has a lifetime of experience in the realm of identity. This long awaited book will greatly add to the important field of knowing our identity in Christ. Finally, as you read this book, the real you can come to the surface.

JONATHAN WELTON
Best-Selling Author & Director of The Welton Academy

Ministry schools, leaders, and Bible study teachers all need this book! It is an identity transformer! People want to operate in the supernatural, but mental strongholds stop them in their tracks. Negative self-talk sabotages people—especially young people who are passionate about God. I have known Linda for fifteen years, and as Senior Pastor of an apostolic training center, I highly recommend her ministry. She is very prophetic and gifted. *The Real You* is an effective identity training guide.

JOHN ROSS
Senior Pastor and Apostolic Leader of Cloud Nine Worship Center
San Diego, California

CONTENTS

BEGIN YOUR TRANSFORMATION HERE...

Wouldn't it be great to know what God says about you? How much peace would it bring to your life if your inner thought life expressed God's thoughts about you throughout the day? No more negative thoughts creeping in and sabotaging your dreams. No more self-talk trying to tear you down. No, now you're connected to God, and your own thoughts are speaking what He says—not what the world says.

How about knowing who you are and having direction as to what to do with your life? When you restructure your thought-life and begin believing your real identity—*The Real You*—you enter God's limitless world. God designed *you* for living in His limitless, supernatural world where the unhealed are healed, where your dreams and visions bear fruit, and where you speak with a profound authority that brings down signs and wonders from heaven to earth.

Our thought lives are an on-going battle. Most minds run wild, letting any and all thoughts come in and set up camp—for a lifetime. More often than not, these thoughts produce a very inaccurate picture of who we are. The supernatural transformation of our lives moves in slow motion because most of us are not very proactive in changing our mindsets. We read the Word, even listen to messages, but when it comes right down to it, most of us have a secret thought life that fights us tooth and nail on firmly *believing* God. There is a spiritual dimension behind your silent inner dialogue. Sure, you are seated in heavenly realms. But consider this: Do you *actively* posture yourself there?

You are a supernatural being living in a physical world. Many of us move in and out of the spirit realm without being aware of it. Knowing your true identity opens you up to revelatory realms where engaging with the supernatural is a normal way of life. An unlimited supply of God's power and grace and mercy courses through your veins. When you are not conformed to the patterns and limitations of this world, your entire being transforms to function more naturally in signs and wonders. *The Real You* has fierce faith and prays fierce prayers. You get out of the boat and expect God to show up right here, right now. God's view of you is vast. We often live from a limited perspective based on our limited circumstances. All of this will begin to change as you delve into your true identity with God!

Using This Activation Manual

The Real You is an eleven-week high level identity training with two books: *The Real You— Believing Your True Identity* and *The Real You Activation Manual*. I also strongly suggest you watch *The Real You* teaching DVDs that accompany each chapter. *The Real You* DVD's contain eleven short videos of Linda Breitman teaching on the topic of the week. In your first meeting (if you are in a group), read out loud *Begin Your Transformation Here!* and answer the discussion questions. The long list of *sub-fruit* from the initial fruit is extensive.

For the next ten weeks, you will read one chapter per week from the book. It is important to read the chapter right away because each week you will be *posturing* in the topic covered. Posturing means to take a posture or stance from God's perspective on a topic and verbally proclaim it. For ten weeks you will be posturing on a facet of your true identity in Christ. Every morning and every night, you will say topical Scriptures that have been personalized for you to speak them in first person. Posturing is vital! By posturing, you are being proactive in renewing your mind and agreeing with your identity.

IMPORTANT: If you do not have time to read the opening section for the chapter right away, go straight to the posturing verses and start speaking them twice a day. The goal is to posture in each topic at least twice a day for seven days. The identity declarations will become absorbed into your heart and mind. Many who have immersed themselves in this Activation Manual carry the verses with them and posture throughout the day.

Each week, complete the Activation Manual assignment for the corresponding chapter. The manual contains fill-in-the-blank questions as well as writing your own personal response to something you learned. You will have a Posturing section, a Before Posturing prayer, and an Activation section to *activate* the target of each chapter more fully in your life. Each chapter closes with a Prayer and a Heavenly Word. Once you have answered the questions in each chapter, turn to the answer section at the back of the book and compare your answers.

The Real You will help you to know in your *knower* who you really are—who God says you are. Speaking the Word of God is a far cry from speaking worldly affirmations. The Word is living and active, sharper than any two-edged sword, judging the thoughts and motives of the heart. As a believer, the Truth is already *resident* in you. Jesus is *in* you. You are pulling on the Truth *inside* you and bringing it to the forefront. You are aligning your entire being—especially your mind—with God's view of you. So, don't think speaking identity verses is having words from the outside come in to your mind. Truth that is hidden deep inside you is coming out! To become more aligned with God's thoughts and intentions for you is to cooperate with His transformation process. You are agreeing with a transformed life. Romans 12:2, Ephesians 4:23, and 2 Corinthians 10:3-5 are primary verses instructing us to pull down strongholds of wrong thinking and take concerted action to change the way we think. Why is our identity so vague to us? How did we lose it? To find out the answers to these questions, we have to go back to the beginning.

How Did We Get Here?

I've been teaching on building the true identity of a believer for a long time. People always wonder, how did we get here? How did we lose our identity? Or better yet, how was our identity stolen? To understand how our self-image became so distorted, we have to go all the way back to Genesis and the Garden of Eden. Here we find out how we lost our identity, how the initial fruit produced from the fall of humankind affected our lives, and how we see God's plan for restoration. If you have the DVDs that go with this book, watch the Introduction Video now. I present a brief in-depth teaching on how we lost our identity.

Two Trees in the Garden

There were two trees in the Garden of Eden: the tree of life and the tree of the knowledge of good and evil. In Genesis 2:9b, we are introduced to the trees:

In the middle of the garden were the tree of life and the tree of the knowledge of good and evil.

In Genesis 2:16-17, the Lord God told Adam he must not eat from the tree of the knowledge of good and evil.

And the Lord God commanded the man, "You are free to eat from any tree in the garden; but you must not eat from the tree of the knowledge of good and evil, for when you eat of it you will surely die."

Adam and Eve enjoyed close friendship with God. They knew they were loved and accepted. They were not concerned about what to wear or toiling for food. It is important to note that Genesis 2:25 states:

*The man and his wife were both naked, and **they felt no shame**.*

In the next scene, we find the serpent offered Eve the fruit from the forbidden tree. The words of God were twisted. She fell for his deception and ate the fruit. She gave some to her husband, and he ate it. Immediately, they realized they were naked. In Genesis 3:10, Adam said,

*I heard you [God] in the garden, and I was **afraid** because I was **naked**; so I **hid**.*

The result of eating from the tree of the knowledge of good and evil was that three initial fruit were birthed:

- Fear
- Shame
- Loss of Identity

Each initial fruit represents kingdoms contrary to God and leads to more deceptive and destructive fruit. The long list of *sub-fruit* from fear, shame, and loss of identity is extensive. As you learn how this insidious tree operates, you will see places in the tree where you have allowed yourself to live. These are strongholds in your life. Many of them have been life-long struggles. We inherit this fruit from the fall of man. Even so, each stronghold can be dismantled and destroyed.

The first fruit on the list is fear. Fear endeavors to immobilize us. When we look at circumstances that are difficult, we feel hopeless. It becomes difficult to believe we have a future. We fear things like rejection, abandonment, failure, success, loneliness, and betrayal. We fear the future, losing a job, not having enough, financial lack, health problems, death—either ours or that of those we love—and the list goes on. Can you identify with any of these? Fear keeps us from living in God's world and seeing ourselves from God's perspective.

Let's look at shame. Shame is tricky. It produces insecurity, insignificance, confusion, depression, isolation, loneliness, condemnation, self-hatred, and hopelessness. Because we feel unworthy and bad inside, we are compelled to strive for acceptance through performance and perfectionism. Shame also brings thoughts of suicide. Gnarly, huh? Shame makes us feel like we are never good enough.

Every person's identity is going to be challenged. Jesus' was. Satan challenged the identity of Jesus in the wilderness for forty days. Loss of identity means not knowing God's original intent for who we really are. This loss prevents us from enjoying an intimate relationship with God. It keeps us from growing in our relationships with other people. It pulls us into the cycle of blame. We can become very critical when we don't know who we are. We get defensive and put up walls of protection to keep everyone out so they don't know how we don't know who we are. Fruit that grows under the umbrella of loss of identity includes rejection, abandonment, uncertainty, panic, lack of direction, and feeling like we are of little or no value.

The accuser lives in this tree. He continually accuses us and drives us deeper into the tree of the knowledge of good and evil. He deceives us into thinking if we perform better, we will be accepted. Grace is nowhere to be found. A religious spirit makes us strive to be perfect. If we are perfect, we will be loved. The tree is rooted in legalism and bondage.

The list of *sub-fruit* from the initial fruit of fear, shame, and loss of identity is extensive and produces much more sub-fruit than I have listed here. But there is a way out. The Garden also holds the tree of *life*. The beautiful, glorious tree of life! The fruit from this tree flourishes with love, acceptance, joy, provision, freedom, healing, righteousness, peace, hope, and a wondrous, intimate, deeply personal relationship with God! The breath of God blows through the tree of life with constant revelation and encouragement. This tree is rooted in wild, glorious freedom.

Moving Over to the Tree of Life

Like most of us, you have probably recognized in which tree you spend most of your thought life. I can pretty much guess that you find yourself mostly in the tree of the knowledge of good and evil. Many believers do. Even leaders struggle with this tree. But you can switch trees. After we accept Jesus as Lord and Savior, we are to renew our minds so that our thoughts are aligned with heaven. That means we can *change the way we think* by letting go of the patterns of how the world thinks and starting to think with the mind of Christ. *The Real You* trains you how to "no longer conform to the patterns of this world, but be transformed by the renewing of your mind" (Romans 12:2). Transforming our thoughts is how we begin. To fully win the battle for our minds, we must confront the atmosphere around us. We must confront the spirit realm. Often a demonic spirit is behind each fruit from the fall. In breaking free, three actions are critical:

1. Break the agreement with the lie you have believed
2. Be pro-active in renewing your mind
3. Confront the spirit realm by breaking the demonic hold connected to bad fruit

For example, a *spirit* of fear is associated with thoughts and feelings of fear. To address the *thought*, you may proclaim from 2 Timothy 1:6,

God has not given me a spirit of fear, but of power and of love and of a sound mind.

And then to address the *spirit realm*, you can stand in the authority given to you by Jesus in Luke 10:19 and proclaim,

In Jesus' name, I command the spirit of fear to leave me!

The Real You Activation Manual equips you to live from the tree of life and activate your multi-faceted identity in Christ in power and authority. You will learn to see yourself more consistently from the heavenly realms position where you are seated. The goal is for you to strengthen your true identity and then enjoy doing all the fun, exhilarating things Jesus did! Isn't it about time? Jesus said, "Anyone who has faith in me will do what I have been doing. He will do even greater things than these…" (John 14:12).

Discussion Questions

1. What kinds of things do you say to yourself throughout the day? What do you think God thinks about you?

2. Read Romans 12:2. What is this verse instructing us to do? What happens when you do it? What does not being conformed to the patterns of this world mean to you?

3. According to the second paragraph in *Begin Your Transformation Here*, when our minds are renewed we enter more fully into God's supernatural world. Why do you think renewing the mind activates the supernatural in our lives? What kinds of supernatural things would you like to see more of in your life?

4. Read John 14:12. What did Jesus do that you will do? What do you think are the greater things?

5. Read Ephesians 4:22-24. What are we instructed to do? How can we do this?

6. Read 2 Corinthians 10:3-5. Discuss the meaning of this verse in your own words.

notes...

ALIGN YOUR THOUGHTS WITH HEAVEN

Aligning Your Thoughts to Fully Reflect the Mindset of Heaven

Being aware of the thoughts we think is the first step toward establishing our true identity. Our thoughts are either in agreement with God, or they are not. Many of us want to embrace who God says we are, but we are challenged with negative mindsets that have been with us for years. The Bible speaks of our real identity—and it is not negative. Our identity is full of hopes and dreams and freedom. Knowing our identity brings tremendous authority and breakthrough, impacting not only our lives but also the lives of others. Detrimental self-talk hinders us from attaining those dreams and hinders the supernatural transformation of a renewed mind. In this chapter, we will begin the transformation process by changing what and how we think.

It's time to align our thoughts with heaven!

1. READ PHILIPPIANS 4:8.

a) Paul lists eight topics and tells us to think about these things. In other words, stop with the negative thinking, and intentionally think on these truths. What eight things does Paul urge us to meditate on?

b) God understands that we face difficult situations that cause us to feel anxious. When we are anxious, our thought lives becomes troublesome. In the verses preceding Philippians 4:8, we see how to deal with negative thinking. Read Philippians 4:4–7. God knows our emotions can try to get the best of us during difficult times, so we are first encouraged to rejoice—and rejoice always. Personally, I believe we are instructed to rejoice in the face of trouble because this contrary action assaults anxiety with the opposite spirit and weakens its hold on us. Next, anxiety is addressed. Feelings of anxiety come knocking at everyone's door. According to this passage, how are we directed to respond to anxiety?

c) The first word on the list in verse 8 is *true*. Using the Bible as your guide, write three things you know are true.

d) How dramatically would it affect your outlook on life if you meditated on these things?

a) If someone were to crawl inside your mind today, what thoughts would they discover?

b) All of us have to fight off negative thoughts that try to limit us. What are the most discouraging thoughts with which you wrestle?

How do you deal with them? Or do you try?

What are your most positive thoughts?

c) The Holy Spirit downloads ideas and dreams into our spirit. He stirs up places of creativity and then pours in strategies so we can attain our aspirations. Yet most of our dreams go unrealized because our self-talk negates them. What things do you say to yourself that negate your dreams and goals?

d) What is the key to uncovering the real you?

e) Complete the following sentence: The mind is a _____,
a _____, where thoughts are constantly fighting for_____.

f) What happens when we align our thoughts with heaven?

g) Do your most dominant thoughts depict an accurate picture of who God says you are?

a) What happens when we enter into a life walk with Jesus?

b) According to Romans 12:2, what is the overall result of renewing our minds?

c) Who does the renewing? _____. We take deliberate action to pull out a lifetime of _____, _____ thoughts and _____ them with what God says is _____ about us.

d) A renewed mind blows the lid off _____ thinking. A renewed mind is not _____ in its thinking.

e) Did you ever consider that renewing your mind means you are more fully cooperating with God's transformational work in your life?

f) In what ways have you experienced your mind being renewed?

g) What did your thought life look like before Jesus came into your life?

h) Read 2 Corinthians 10:5. Every thought contrary to God's truth can be

_____, _____,

and _____ with what is true.

a) Aligning your mind with heaven is a _____ choice.

b) Know one thing for sure: You _____ have to accept every thought
that comes drifting along. You can _____ thoughts.

How will this affect your attitude toward your thought life?

c) By posturing with God's Word, you are _____ re-wiring your
thinking by _____ and _____ reality from
heaven's perspective.

d) How do we begin building up the *real* you?

e) As you declare these personalized verses about your thought life, you will be
_____ with lies and _____
the spirit realm. You will begin _____ , _____,
and _____ powerful mindsets—mindsets that are taken directly
from _____.

5. POSTURING: TAKING CHARGE OF MY THOUGHTS.

Posturing is the heart of this study. Without posturing in each section, you will not experience the transformation of a renewed mind. To speak these verses everyday takes discipline and perseverance. I suggest you place *The Real You* next to your bed at night. Speak them right before bed and first thing upon rising.

a) Which three verses strengthen you the most?

b) Which three verses are you having difficulty saying?

Renewing your mind by posturing in the Word of God establishes and builds your real identity. In the first activation, you will begin learning how to posture. To posture is to position yourself. It means you are taking a specific stance. When you posture in God's Word, you position yourself to be in agreement with God. You are no longer aligning yourself with worldly thinking, but rather you are aligning yourself with God's perspective.

It is vital that your deep inner dialog reflects God's Word. You are not exchanging one earthbound mindset for another earthbound mindset. When you speak God's Word, you are stepping into agreement with heaven.

Take the posturing verses you just read and incorporate them into your daily life. You are the one who renews your mind. You take up the sword of the Spirit, which is the Word of God, and proclaim it. This is a week-long activation—and it is the most powerful of all. If you do nothing else—just posture.

Your assignment is this: Read the verses first thing in the morning when you get up and again right before you go to bed. Decide right now you are going to make this your priority. Carry the verses with you and speak them throughout the day. There is no such thing as proclaiming God's Word too much. I will tell you right now that you will be challenged to give up, quit, or simply forget. Recognize the warfare. All the forces of hell want you not to speak verses that build your true identity. It takes effort and perseverance. Dig down deep and tap into a warrior mindset! Always remember that you are in a war. And the battle is for your mind!

ACTIVATION ONE

a) As you renew your mind this week by reading the verses every day for seven days, first thing in the morning and right before you go to bed, keep track of how you feel. Can you feel a difference from posturing this week?

b) As you posture, you may find difficulty fully believing and even speaking some of the verses. When this happens, you most likely have believed a lie. A lie is a wrong mindset. The lie will pretty much be the opposite of your proclamation. This is a place in your mind that needs to be renewed. Choose one verse that you are having a hard time accepting as being true for you. Write the verse.

Ask the Holy Spirit "What is the lie I accepted as truth that kept me from believing this verse?" Maybe you have believed you can't change the way you think or that you just automatically think negative thoughts. Or you still believe negative things someone said to you. Write down the lie the Holy Spirit shows you.

Ask God to forgive you for believing the lie. Verbally break the agreement you have had with the lie. You can say something like, "Lord, I am sorry for believing the lie. It has kept me from believing Your Word. In Jesus' name, I break my agreement with that lie, and I command any demonic spirit attached to the lie to leave me now! Now, I believe _____."

Write the verse again in your own words.

You have begun demolishing a stronghold and replaced a wrong mindset with a mindset aligned with your true identity.

Often, there is an injured place in our hearts where the lie came in. You don't have to even identify the injury for God to heal your heart. Just ask Him to heal you. Say, "Lord, heal the injured place in my heart where the lie came in."

Sit quietly a moment. Accept that He is healing your heart and mind. This process guides you through specific actions you can take to renew your mind! You are purposefully pulling down a demonic stronghold and planting truth in your mind. You will begin feeling differently about verses with which you have struggled. Sometimes a renewal in your mind happens quickly, and sometimes the change takes place over time. Do this process with any verse that you finddifficult to accept. Blowing up strongholds requires a conscious effort on your part, but you can do this. God has equipped you to be an overcomer.

In the space below, jot down other verses you have a problem accepting and believing.

ACTIVATION THREE

c) Take out some paper, set a timer, and for five minutes, write whatever comes to mind. Write your thoughts without stopping. Write the positive things you say to yourself as well as the negative things. Take a look. Writing your thoughts will give you an indication as to what you tend to think about when you're not really thinking about what you're thinking. I urge you not to skip over this Activation. It will open your eyes to some of your inner thoughts. When I am mentoring a person, I read his or her written thoughts. It gives me a clearer insight into the person's thought life.

What themes do you see?

ACTIVATION FOUR

d) Look up 2 Corinthians 10:3-5 in a few different translations. What is the Holy Spirit revealing to you through this passage?

e) In the space provided below, draw two people. Draw one person with a renewed mind and one person with old mindsets. Draw how each person looks on the outside and on the inside.

f) What do you see? What are the major similarities, and what are the major differences between these people?

g) Which one reflects the real you?

7. PRAYER: Transforming My Thought Life

a) According to Ephesians 2:6, we are seated together with Christ. Where are we seated?

b) How does this affect the way you see yourself?

8. HEAVENLY WORD

a) What is your mind a gateway to?

b) _____ and _____
are in the power of the tongue.

notes...

Your New Identity

Believing and Declaring Exactly Who God Says You Are

This chapter is all about YOU! It's all about your new identity—believing and declaring who God says you really are. No matter what you may think about yourself right now, know that God has a plan to transform your mind one victorious thought at a time!

1. READ ROMANS 12:2.

a) Rewrite the verse in your own words.

b) The definition of *renew* is taken from *Vine's Expository Dictionary of Biblical Words*. Write the definition of *renew* in the space below and your thoughts about it.

c) Look up *renew* in a regular dictionary. What definitions seem to reflect the intention of Romans 12:2?

2. AFTER READING THE FIRST TWO PARAGRAPHS IN THE CHAPTER, ANSWER THE FOLLOWING QUESTIONS.

a) What questions like "Who am I? Where am I going? What's the meaning of life?" have you ever asked yourself?

b) For most of your life, what has defined your identity?

c) How do you grow solid in your real identity?

a) The devil does not want you to _____ who you really are. And _____ on it. And _____ it.

Write a prayer, telling God that from this day forward you make the choice to learn more about your true identity in Christ and to firmly *believe* it.

b) Read Luke 4:1-13. What was satan challenging?

c) How did Jesus counter satan's demonic accusations?

d) According to the text, "as you follow His [Jesus'] lead, _____ your identity from _____, tremendous _____ will rise up inside of you as you step into who you really are—the *real* you."

e) Why do you think there is such an ongoing battle for your identity?

4. NOW READ PARAGRAPHS SEVEN, EIGHT, AND NINE.

a) The *you* God meant for you to be is bold, confident, tender, and strong. God says that the *real* you is _____. The *real* you is _____. You have _____ and _____ from God, and He wants you to _____ them. You have a _____, and you have _____.

Right now stop and declare all of these qualities over yourself! How does that make you feel?

b) In the space below write out Ephesians 4:23 from the Amplified Bible and describe what stands out in this verse to you.

c) What is the best way to deal with self-defeating thoughts?

5. POSTURING: MY NEW IDENTITY. READ THROUGH THE POSTURING VERSES, SAYING EACH VERSE OUT LOUD.

a) Which three verses do you have the least amount of difficulty saying?

b) Which three verses do you have the most difficulty saying?

6. IDENTITY ACTIVATIONS: New Identity. Read through and follow the steps in each activation.

ACTIVATION 1

a) The first activation in every chapter is on *posturing*. Posturing tears down wrong mindsets and immerses you in your true identity. *Speaking* the verses is the most important and most powerful of the activations. Decide right now that you are going to go for it and establish the habit of posturing. The transformation posturing produces is drastic. But you can do it. You *can* renew your mind. Your assignment is this: *Speak* the verses for the next seven days—once in the morning and again right before bed.

Also, continue speaking the verses from chapter 1 at least once every couple days. It's not unusual for me to proclaim quite a few different topics at a time. I carry the verses with me so I can speak them randomly throughout the day. No one can renew your mind but you. It takes diligence, but *you* can do this. Ask God for the grace you need to renew your mind. These posturing verses are designed to build up your *overall* identity in Christ. Subsequent chapters will address more specific aspects of identity.

What changes are you noticing in yourself as you take time to posture?

b) *The Real You* will train you to identify, confront, and transform wrong mindsets. This can be very, very challenging because a wrong mindset is a lie you have believed as a truth. To build your true identity—the identity God has for you—you must dismantle these lies. Some lies will be very obvious and others will be subtler.

Activation two will be the same throughout the study. By the time you complete the last chapter, you will be equipped to recognize wrong mindsets and replace them with everything God says is true about you and about Himself. Follow the steps below:

Posturing in Scripture is a vital part of renewing your mind. Sometimes, when we declare a verse, we have a hard time getting the words out of our mouths. Not fully believing the verse for ourselves indicates that we believe something contrary to the verse. We have believed a *lie* and established a wrong mindset in our thinking. The lie may have entered your life at an early age when harsh or unkind words were spoken to you. Sometimes, when traumatic experiences happen to us, we make an inner decision that is in direct opposition to what God says is true. Sometimes, we arbitrarily decide something is true because we don't know better. Lies are strongholds; they can be demolished. You do not have to live with lies—no matter how long ago they were erected.

Write down a verse you have difficulty believing.

Ask the Holy Spirit, "What is the lie I accepted as truth that kept me from believing this verse?" Write down that lie. Remember, a lie is a wrong mindset.

Ask God to forgive you for believing the lie. Verbally break the agreement you have had with the lie. Say, "Lord, I am sorry for believing the lie. It prevented me from believing Your Word. In Jesus' name, I break my agreement with that deceptive lie. The bondage is broken! From now on, I believe _____."

Write the verse again in your own words.

Most of the time, lies lodge in our being along with hurt. Something happened that wounded us, and we bought into a lie. You may or may not be aware of a hurt place. Don't go dredging up possible hurts. He heals us even when we don't know exactly what the hurt is and where it came from. By faith, say, "Lord, heal the injured place in my heart where the lie came in." Sit quietly and let God speak to your heart. Let the truth soak in; let it permeate your body, soul, and spirit.

ACTIVATION 3

c) People generally base their identity on performance. Worth is based on how well you measure up to everyone else.

What makes you see yourself as successful?

Ask the Holy Spirit to show you your true identity from God's perspective. Write down what the Holy Spirit revealed.

Write how God defines your identity using the posturing verses.

ACTIVATION 4

d) You don't become who God says you are—you *believe* who God says you are. Jesus didn't try to become the Son of God—He was the Son of God. Your real identity resides *in* you right now. Your performance does not determine your identity. God loves you the same, even if you do not do anything else for Him. God loves you because that is what He does. He so loved the world that He sent His Son, not because we had done anything to deserve it. So many times when we mess up, we think God is mad or that He will withhold His love from us. Do you feel that God loves you apart from performance?

e) When Jesus asked the question, "Who do you say I am?" (Matthew 16:15), He was asking them if they knew His true identity. Simon Peter replied, "You are the Christ, the son of the living God." Jesus emphasized that Peter did not receive this crucial, high-level revelation from man. The only reason Peter had the revelation of Jesus' identity was because it was revealed to Peter by God the Father—the same One who reveals *your* identity. You find your true identity from God the Father—not from man. Just as Jesus did.

I feel God is asking us the same question, "Who do you say you are?" So, who do you say you are? Go ahead and answer.

7. PRAYER: My Identity in Christ

a) After you read the prayer, add a few more lines of your own.

8. HEAVENLY WORD: Receive the words that your Heavenly Father is saying to your heart.

a) Write down key phrases that encourage you.

notes...

notes...

TRANSFORMED INTO HIS LIKENESS

Embracing the Transforming Power of Christ that Is at Work Within You

Everyday we are transforming more and more into the likeness of Christ. As we draw near to Him and learn of Him, His character grows larger in us. This is our destiny—to be like Him, to move like Him, to sound like Him, and to touch like Him. Slow down, close your eyes, and tune in to the transforming power of Christ. Can you sense it? In this very moment, God is transforming you from the inside out!

I. TAKE A LOOK AT THE FIRST FIVE PARAGRAPHS IN CHAPTER 3 OF THE BOOK.

a) What is the definition of *transformed*?

b) According to 2 Corinthians 3:18, we reflect what we behold. Into what image are you being transformed?

c) The Greek word *metamorphoo* means to transform. We derive the word _____ from *metamorphoo*, which means a _____ of form or structure.

d) Read Matthew 17:1-2. What happened to Jesus when He was transformed on the Mount of Transfiguration?

e) You are in a constant state of metamorphosis. In what ways have you changed since you became a Christian?

In what ways have others seen a transformation in your life?

f) As the power of God's Word works on the deep places of your heart, you exhibit more and more of His _____ and _____.
Your _____ will shine with His glory—from the inside out!

What godly qualities would you like to have more of in your life?

g) What three verses use the word *metamorphoo*?

In each verse, how was the word translated?

2. MANY PEOPLE IN THE BIBLE EXHIBITED EXTRAORDINARY CHARACTERISTICS THAT DEMONSTRATED HOW THEY WERE BEING RADICALLY TRANSFORMED INTO THE LIKENESS OF CHRIST.

a) According to the chapter, what did Joshua demonstrate?

b) What did the apostle Paul demonstrate?

c) Joseph?

d) Jael?

e) King David?

f) Deborah?

g) Peter?

h) What other people in the Bible demonstrated qualities reflecting godly character? List a few people and the qualities they exhibited.

i) If you could be like any character in the Bible, who would you want to be like and why?

3. READ JOHN 14:12.

a) What a great promise Jesus gives us in this verse! If we believe in Him, what will we do?

a) Describe the eternal now.

b) When you received Jesus as your Lord and Savior, you received a transfusion of His _____ nature.

c) Your identity is already established, but you _____ in character.

d) Something significant occurs when we connect with the _____ of the _____ that has already happened inside and _____ its fruit.

e) What do you have in you right now?

5. POSTURING: I AM TRANSFORMING. SLOWLY READ THROUGH THE POSTURING VERSES, KEEPING IN MIND THE FOLLOWING QUESTIONS:

a) Which three verses are your favorites?

b) Are you struggling with any of the verses? Which ones?

As you posture everyday, what changes are you beginning to see in your life?

6. IDENTITY ACTIVATIONS: Transforming into His Likeness

ACTIVATION 1

a) Before continuing, read the first activation in chapter 3 of the book.

Declaring the Posturing verses is really soaking your whole being in your true identity. It is the primary key for aligning yourself with God's heart and for bringing forth Kingdom mindsets. Posturing takes effort and diligence, but the payoff is enormous. For one week, speak the verses in this section twice a day—beginning now.

ACTIVATION 2

b) Every week, the first two activations are the same, and thus hit the same target. I urge you to jump into these activations full force. Don't think that you've already done it before. Each week contains fresh proclamations, and new lies will need to be dismantled each week. Persevere. Follow the steps below:

Choose one verse you are having a hard time fully believing and bring it before the Lord. Which verse did you choose?

Ask the Lord to show you why you are having a hard time with this verse. What lie did God reveal to you?

Repentance is the door to freedom. Ask God to forgive you for believing the lie. Verbally break the agreement you have had with the lie. Say, "Lord, I am sorry for believing the lie. It has kept me from believing Your Word. In Jesus' name, I break my agreement with that lie and command any demonic spirit attached to the lie to leave me now! The bondage is broken! From now on, I believe _____."

Write the verse again in your own words.

Ask God to heal the injured place where the lie came in. Write your thoughts about this process.

ACTIVATION 3

c) Godly character is developed over time as we experience both trials and victories. With every breath, we recognize more of God's love and grace. Write down five godly characteristics of King David that you want to see activated in your life.

Whether you are in a study group, or doing this on your own, anoint yourself with oil and ask the Holy Spirit to develop these qualities in you. Write down a prayer that expresses your desire to walk out these qualities.

ACTIVATION 4

d) Read 2 Corinthians 3:18 in a few different translations. Rewrite the verse using your own words.

ACTIVATION 5

e) On post-it notes, write your favorite posturing decrees found in this chapter and place them on your bathroom mirror. You will see them there regularly and have a few extra moments to ponder them! Which verses are you going to put on post-it notes this week?

Why did you pick these verses?

7. TRANSFORMATION PRAYER

a) Add your own words to the prayer.

8. HEAVENLY WORD

a) According to the Word, what happens when Jesus appears?

notes...

TOTALLY ACCEPTED AND HIGHLY VALUED

Shedding Performance and Embracing a Lifestyle of Total Acceptance in God

In order to live the full, abundant, exciting life God desires for us, we must understand who we are in Him. We are precious to Him, and He will stop at nothing to help us see just how valuable we are! The following questions will help you see how deeply God loves you, how important it is to love yourself, and how much the body of Christ needs you.

I. READ THE STORY ABOUT MICHELLE IN THE FIRST PARAGRAPH OF CHAPTER 4.

Insert your name in the passage and read those encouraging statements over yourself. Take your time, nice and slow. Let these words really soak into your heart. The words spoken over Michelle are true about you. Let them heal any drops of rejection. Even if it's just a drop, it's too much. If these words bring to mind any experiences from the past, ask the Holy Spirit to bring healing to your heart.

a) Were the words easy or difficult for you to receive? Do you believe them?

b) Define *valuable*.

a) Remembering a time of rejection or abandon doesn't feel very good, but through this study you will find healing. Describe a time you experienced rejection or felt abandoned.

b) The first sentence in paragraph three asks you to verbalize three statements that reflect the *real* you. Go ahead and say them right now. Many of us have had a hard time believing these truths. As you speak them, how confident are you in really believing what you are saying? Circle one.

| 1 | 2 | 3 | 4 | 5 | 6 | 7 | 8 | 9 | 10 |

Not Very Confident   Very Confident

c) When you boldly proclaim God's perspective on a matter, there is a confrontation between God's Kingdom and the demonic kingdom. Demonic strongholds do not want to give up ground without a fight. When you persevere and proclaim truth over yourself, strongholds that have held on tight from as long ago as childhood, weaken and fall. Let's go for it! Say once more, "I am valuable. God loves me and accepts me."

Do this slowly and purposefully. Think about each stated truth. Open your heart and think of each statement as a wave washing over you. Be washed with the water of the Word. Are these words resonating in you heart? How so?

Are there any voices piping up, saying something to you that contradicts these truths?

d) All of us want to feel accepted. We want to be loved just the way we are. The One who knows you more completely than anyone else does just that: He loves you and accepts you. Close your eyes for a minute and really think about this question: What does it mean to you to know God accepts you?

e) Our ability to grow in the talents God has given us corresponds directly to our own acknowledgment of _____.

f) Even our capacity to love others is wholly related to how much we _____ and _____ ourselves.

g) Read Mark 12:33. Why does Jesus include "love your neighbor as yourself" in the commandments?

h) How we treat people is determined by our self-worth. Our self-worth is solidified through believing _____.

i) Our concept of self-worth is based on _____ our identity. As we know who we are in God's heart, we find _____ and _____, and only then do we really know how to live.

a) Close your eyes and ask the Holy Spirit to show you upon what worldly standards you have based you self-worth. Describe what you sense He is revealing to you.

b) What happens when we compare ourselves to others?

c) True self-worth has nothing to do with _____. It has to do with seeing yourself through _____.

a) Remember, you are in the process of transforming into that beautiful butterfly. You *will* be transformed into His likeness, and the day will come when you will completely see yourself through God's eyes. Right now say, "I am going to see myself through God's eyes. My self-worth is not based on my performance."

b) Our true value is founded on what two truths?

c) Read Matthew 13:44–46. In this passage, the merchant represents _____. He places such enormous _____ on you that He sacrificed _____ for you. What does God treasure most?

a) Why does the body of Christ need you?

b) What does the price we are willing to pay for an item reflect about the item?

c) Read 1 Peter 1:18-19. The world places a high value on silver and gold, but what did God use as payment to redeem you?

d) What does that say about you?

6. READ THROUGH PARAGRAPH TEN.

a) As you proclaim these truths, what do you dismantle and what are you building on?

a) Which three verses encourage you the most?

b) Do you have difficulty fully believing any of the verses? Which ones?

8. IDENTITY ACTIVATIONS: You Are the Pearl of Great Price

ACTIVATION 1

a) A glorious facet of your true identity is knowing down deep that you are totally accepted by God. Believing you are highly valued crushes jealousy and inferiorities. Replacing these old mindsets requires posturing in new, true mindsets with purpose. You are breaking off words that you have spoken about yourself. You are breaking off words others have spoken over you—perhaps from childhood. This is a big deal! When you posture, you are addressing the spirit realm around you as well as renewing your mind.

You are also posturing for a life of supernatural signs, miracles, and wonders to operate in and through *you*! This inner transformation will manifest outwardly. Jesus said, "And these signs will accompany those who believe" (Mark 16:17-18). What are those signs? Signs of a transformed and supernatural life. Take time this week and read these verses over yourself everyday, multiple times a day—particularly first thing in the morning and right before bed. You will dream with these verses on your mind! What are your thoughts about posturing in new mindsets?

b) Over the course of our lives many of us have been told things that were hurtful and devaluing. These destructive words then replayed in our minds over and over again, creating a stronghold. As we discover our true value in God, these old negative voices clash with God's truth. Verbalizing our real worth and value is difficult for many. This chapter is life-changing. Yet, the Scriptures are true: You are highly valued.

If you had difficulty reading any of the posturing verses from this section, you have probably believed a lie about yourself. Right now, God can free your spirit from that lie, and bring healing and value to your heart.

Choose one verse you are having difficulty believing.

What is the lie that hindered you from believing the truth?

Get quiet with God. Ask God to forgive you for believing the lie. Verbally break the agreement you have had with the lie. Say, "Lord, I am sorry for believing the lie. It has kept me from believing Your Word. In Jesus' name, I break my agreement with that lie and command any demonic spirit attached to the lie to leave me now! The bondage is broken! From now on, I believe _____."

Write the verse again in your own words.

Ask God to heal your heart where the lie came in. Relax. Soak in God's presence, accepting that you have great value, worth, and significance in Him. You are who He says you are, not who the world says you are.

ACTIVATION 3

c) Look right into your eyes in a mirror several times this week. Point to yourself and say, "You are accepted by God. God created you and planned you! Your worth and your value are based on what God says is true about you—and nothing else! He loves you way beyond what you can even imagine!"

What thoughts and feelings came up as you declared those truths to yourself in the mirror?

Was it difficult? Did it feel good?

Do you feel you are getting stronger in your identity? How so?

ACTIVATION 4

d) Romans 8 is a powerful chapter in the Bible that focuses on following the leading of the Holy Spirit in our daily lives and being confident of God's love. When you are feeling down, you are most likely not feeling loved, but rather judging yourself with a harsh voice of self-criticism. The chapter closes with two powerful verses in Romans 8:38-39, describing God's love for us. His powerful love compels us to know beyond all doubt that He also accepts us.

In your own words, what do these verses tell us about God's love?

ACTIVATION 5

e) When you find yourself having negative thoughts toward someone, you are likely judging this person with the same critical voice with which you have judged yourself. Stop yourself and come up with something that you like about him or her. Okay, in some cases it might be difficult to find something. Maybe you like his or her hair or skin tone! Find *something*! Ask God to pour more love into your heart for people. You can't conjure up this kind of love—He pours it into you. Ask Him and He will! What are you doing? You are silencing that critical voice, and you will probably also begin to notice that you are not being so hard on yourself as well.

Ask the Holy Spirit to show you someone you have recently judged.

Write something positive about him or her.

Create a prayer asking God to help you love that person with His love.

9. PRAYER: You Are the Priceless Treasure

a) Add one more sentence of your own.

10. HEAVENLY WORD

a) What treasures has God placed in you that you already recognize in yourself?

notes...

notes...

COMPLETELY FORGIVEN

Letting Go of Past Mistakes and Learning to Walk in Complete Freedom

Forgiveness is a powerful facet of our identity in Christ. When you asked God to forgive you and become part of your life, you were reconciled to Him! That is miraculous! Just as God has forgiven us, we are to be imitators of God and forgive others. Easy? Jesus knew it would not be easy. The Bible speaks a lot about the challenge of forgiveness. Read through this chapter with an open heart, and let God's loving forgiveness wash over you. It will transform your heart!

1. READ PARAGRAPH ONE OF CHAPTER 5 IN THE BOOK ALONG WITH EPHESIANS 4:32.

a) What does this verse mean to you?

b) Look at the definition of *forgiveness*. Share your thoughts about forgiveness releasing another from an offense.

c) Think of a time when someone forgave you for something you did. How did it make you feel?

a) No matter how big or small—God _____.

b) Define *repentance*.

c) This is a hard-core, serious activation manual. It hits big targets so you can make proclamations that, once and for all, enable you to enter into *freedom*! As a believer in Christ, it's time for you to not only *know* you are forgiven but also to *believe* it. Now you are going to make a very important proclamation. Posture yourself ahead of time so that right after you speak the proclamation you enter into the *no-condemnation zone*! Right now say, "I am forgiven for everything. It's all been washed off, and my slate is made clean." Say, "No more feeling bad and guilty. Jesus has washed it off. I am free from all condemnation!"

Share your reaction to this proclamation. Which parts of the proclamation impacted you the most? Add a few words of your own.

d) When we are hurt, our natural inclination is to _____ or _____ or at least let people know _____ even hate them. In the face of our pain, we take it upon _____ to enforce justice.

e) There's only one problem: Lack of forgiveness _____ and
_____ God's Kingdom of intimacy and power. Period.
It keeps _____ from living in our _____.

f) A heart postured in forgiveness is to

g) Read Romans 12:19-21. What is the primary impact this passage has on you?

h) Fill in the blanks from paragraph five. The judgment seat belongs to _____.
Only He can see the _____. Only He is the righteous judge. It's not your
_____.

i) Okay, take a deep breath. So far, how is this chapter impacting you?

a) Read Matthew 6:14–15. What happens when we don't forgive others?

b) Read Matthew 18:21–35. We see in this illustration the importance of forgiving others. What thoughts does this evoke in you?

c) What does unforgiveness produce?

No _____.

No _____.

No _____.

d) How does the Kingdom work? God heals your heart when you _____
_____ and do what He did for you—_____.
Is it easy? Not always. In _____ you can forgive and receive forgiveness.

e) Does forgiveness justify the wrongdoing?

f) What does forgiveness do?

g) Does forgiveness mean the people who have wronged you are getting off the hook? ____
Who gets *off the hook*? _____When we forgive, we will no longer be in _____ to the person who hurt us.

a) What creeps in when we don't forgive ourselves?

b) In the same way you forgive and release others, you can

Right now say, "Lord, I forgive myself. I choose to forgive myself for _____
_____. No longer will I hold judgments against myself and be so critical of myself. It's over. I *forgive* myself!"

c) What is it like for you to speak forgiveness toward yourself?

d) Read paragraph ten. Forgiving the church is vital! Right now, ask God to show you when people in the church at large have hurt you. Maybe something happened to you before you became a Christian. Maybe something happened recently. Right now, begin the forgiveness process by speaking forgiveness concerning those situations He showed you. Hand your hurt over to God.

What events did He show you that you forgave?

e) Read paragraph eleven. There may be times you feel God has let you down. Perhaps something bad happened—a trauma, perhaps, and you thought God could have stopped it, but He didn't. Did anger toward God begin to grow in your heart? After all the betrayal and injustice Joseph incurred, he recognized God actually used it for good. In Genesis 50:20, to the brothers who had severely harmed him, Joseph said, "You intended to harm me, but God intended it for good to accomplish what is now being done, the saving of many lives."

Joseph realized there was a bigger picture. When we hold an offense concerning God, it means we do not trust Him for the big picture. Having faith in God is to believe He is good and that He loves us—and that He sees the bigger picture that we do not see.

Quietly, look inside and determine if there is even the smallest offense in your heart. This is a big deal. It is one more step of moving into a closer and more personal relationship with God. It is about trusting in who God says He is. If this has stirred something in you, now would be a good time to come clean with God and repent. In the space below, write a personal prayer to God.

5. POSTURING: FORGIVENESS

a) Share some of your favorite verses on the lines below.

6. IDENTITY ACTIVATIONS: SAYING YES TO FORGIVENESS

ACTIVATION I

a) Forgiveness is part of your true identity. You are being transformed into His likeness—and God is a forgiver. The forgiveness posturing verses will lead you into a safe place with God where you can immerse yourself in the forgiveness process. You purposefully posture your heart to forgive. Hold these verses close to your heart and speak them a couple times a day. It will really soften your heart and bring healing to long-time wounds in your heart. Posturing is crucial to renewing old mindsets. Speak these verses twice a day for the next week.

What impact does posturing in forgiveness seem to have on you?

ACTIVATION 2

b) We are never finished with forgiveness. Many of us put our head in the sand and avoid it. We resist forgiving. In Matthew 18:21-22, Jesus was asked how many times we need to forgive: "Then Peter came to Jesus and asked, 'Lord, how many times shall I forgive my brother when he sins against me? Up to seven times?' Jesus answered, 'I tell you, not seven times, but seventy-seven times.'"

Forgiving is not easy for us. Jesus has asked us to do something that is totally contrary to how the world operates—but forgiveness will heal your heart. Offenses come our way with regularity, and our job is to acquire a lifetime posture of forgiveness. The posturing verses you have read aloud require courage. Acknowledging people you need to forgive may reopen old wounds before healing can cover them and restore your soul. Forgiveness liberates *you*. Partnered with God, forgiveness can soak deeper into your heart and become a way of life for you.

Follow the steps below:

Ask the Holy Spirit to show you a person you need to forgive. You very likely have been carrying an offense. Ask the Holy Spirit to show you the person and the offense. What is He revealing to you?

Get quiet for a moment with God. With the Holy Spirit at your side, speak forgiveness toward that person. Remember, this is a starting place. In the next chapter, we will address getting the hurt place in your heart fully healed. Write forgiveness toward this person.

Ask God to forgive you for holding onto an offense. Do this now. Say, "Forgive me for holding onto this offense. I break my agreement with the offense." Next, release that person to God. Say, "I release _____ to You, Lord." Remember, it does not mean that what was done to you was right. You are releasing yourself as you release that person when you break your agreement with the offense. Take your time. When you are ready, speak blessing over the person. Even though this may feel hard, the Holy Spirit is right there with you, helping you. Say, "Lord, I speak blessing over _____. Bless them abundantly."

Write about what just transpired.

Ask, "Lord, heal the place in my heart that was injured from this situation." Sit quietly a moment. The Holy Spirit is working forgiveness in your heart. You are purposefully pulling down a stronghold, and the healing power of forgiveness is at work. You are entering into freedom!

ACTIVATION 3

c) Because of God's ongoing forgiveness, we are not to suffer from condemnation. For this activation, we are taking to heart the fact that 1 John 1:9 is true: "If we confess our sins, He is faithful and just and will forgive us our sins and purify us from all unrighteousness."

There may be situations you have been involved in that you regret—things you've done and things you've said that you regret and need to take to God. Close your eyes and say, "Show me, Lord, where I need Your forgiveness." Quiet your heart a moment, and let Him reveal what you need to see. Then, put it all at the foot of the cross and ask Him to forgive you. What is one place where you found you need God's forgiveness?

If this is the first time you've asked God to forgive you for things you have done in the past, then it may also be time for you to invite Jesus to be Lord of your life. If you accepted Jesus once, but walked away or haven't been living for Him, invite Him back into your life. Re-commit yourself to Jesus. God is calling you and drawing you back into His arms. Right now, quiet your heart and ask Him to come into your life. Say, "Jesus, come live in my heart. I am so sorry for the things I have done that were wrong and against You. Forgive me of all my sins. You gave Your life for me so I could have a deep, close relationship with God. Thank You for dying on the cross for me. I love You, and I belong to You now, Jesus. I am going to live my life for You! Amen."

If you prayed to ask Jesus to come into your life, or if you re-committed your life to Him, this is a glorious day! Share this with your group.

Write your thoughts.

ACTIVATION 4

d) To prepare your heart for this activation, pray "Because Christ forgave me, I will forgive others. I cannot do this apart from You, Lord. I ask You to help me. Help me to forgive."

Ask the Holy Spirit to show you situations in which you were hurt and the people you need to forgive. With His help, create a list. You have already begun the forgiveness process in the second activation. Throughout the week, go through the same process with your list. If you experienced a major trauma, it would be best to get with a mature believer to go through the forgiveness process with you. Here is a guide for you to follow.

1.   Speak forgiveness out loud toward the person you need to forgive. In your own words, choose to forgive them.
2.   Bring all the wrongs under the blood of Jesus.
3.   Ask God to forgive you for holding on to unforgiveness and for holding onto the offense.
4.   Release each person to God.
5.   Speak a blessing over the lives of those whom you have forgiven.
6.   Rest in God's arms of love.

Write about your reaction.

ACTIVATION 5

e) Forgiveness is a process that unfolds and floods our entire being. Once we have forgiven, accusations from the devil can come to taunt us. It is not unusual for the demonic realm to accuse you of not having truly forgiven a person. Nine times out of ten, this is the enemy trying to torment you. Always ask God first about what is going on. He will tell you if there is more forgiveness that needs to take place with someone. Your first step has been to speak forgiveness toward a person. The Lord will work the whole forgiveness process in you, causing it to drop down into your heart.

When accusations come, declare, "Lord, according to Your Word, I have forgiven this person. You helped me with it. I have forgiven _____."

Have you experienced this kind of accusation? Now that you know how to respond, journal your thoughts.

7. PRAYER: Real Forgiveness

Add your own words of agreement to this prayer.

8. HEAVENLY WORD

a) What do you love the best about this Word?

notes...

notes...

A Healed and Restored Heart

Stepping into God's Gentle, Restorative, Healing Power

We long to have a closer relationship with God. We long to grab hold of the truths in His Word. But sometimes—we get stuck. God tenderly uncovers the wounds in our hearts so we can be healed. As healing saturates our broken hearts, we experience a greater understanding of His extravagant love for us and how much He cares about every detail of our lives.

1. READ PSALM 147:3 AND THE FIRST PARAGRAPH IN CHAPTER 6.

a) What is the definition of *heal*?

b) Jesus wants to heal our hearts. What is the first step to having our hearts healed?

c) Joanne fell and literally hit her head. She said "Ouch, that hurts." When have you experienced a painful situation but tried to move on without acknowledging the pain?

a) Our real identity becomes more fully formed as the emotional wounds in our hearts are _____.

Give some examples of different emotional wounds. (Example: rejection, betrayal, etc.)

b) What did Jesus' mission on earth include?

c) Our personal transformation includes the healing of _____. When wounds are not addressed, a life of joy and freedom is _____.

Can you think of wounds in your own life that have hindered a life of joy and freedom for you?

a) Wounds can be healed in different ways. Some wounds require _____ Some require _____. The healing of some wounds hinges on _____. Also breaking off the power of _____ can heal wounds.

b) All wounds require _____ and not keeping the wound as a badge of honor upon which to hang excuses. If you do, you will soon find your _____ by drawing attention to your wound and feeling sorry for yourself. Self-pity is a _____ that entangles you and keeps you bound if you set up camp there. Keep _____ through the healing process. Jesus came to _____.

c) When we play hurtful scenes from the past over and over in our minds, it is a clear indication we are wounded. Ask the Lord to show you how you have hung onto the past and wanted to say, "Look what terrible thing happened to me!" What experiences did He show you?

a) What two emotions are often linked together? _____ and _____.

b) What effect does anger have on us?

c) Fear is a demonic spirit that immobilizes us. Fear keeps us stuck. In what areas do you feel fear has kept you stuck?

5. READ THROUGH *STEPS TOWARD HEALING YOUR HEART.*

a) Saying, "Ouch, that hurt!" is an admission that _____ and you actually became wounded. Admitting the injury is the _____.

b) To initiate the forgiveness process, begin by _____ forgiveness toward the person. The act of forgiving is an _____.

c) If the situation caused you fear or an emotion that persists, you may be dealing with a _____. If fear has been tormenting you, what can you do?

Look up Luke 10:19. What did Jesus give you authority over?

d) God wants to heal your heart. What is the last step you need to take for the healing of your heart?

6. POSTURING: HEALING WOUNDS IN YOUR HEART. THESE POSTURING VERSES ARE POWERFUL! THEY WILL BRING HEALING, COMFORT, AND STRENGTH TO YOUR HEART.

a) What are some of your favorite verses?

b) Which three verses bring the most encouragement and transformation to your heart?

7. IDENTITY ACTIVATIONS: A HEALED HEART

ACTIVATION I

a) Remember it is important to declare the posturing verses over yourself every day, especially during a focused season of receiving healing for your heart. Store these posturing verses close to your heart. They are life, and they are truth. "He sent forth His Word and healed them..." (Psalm 107:20).

Spend time speaking them over yourself every day this week, at least once in the morning and once at night. Don't hesitate to carry them with you to read during work breaks, in between classes, in line at the store—wherever you can. I pray by now you've established a discipline for posturing in God's Word. Continue to say the verses from other chapters as you feel led by the Holy Spirit. You are in a time of renewal. Renewal takes effort and sacrifice. Very likely, you will have to give something up to create the extra time for posturing and renewing your mind. Your true identity is gaining strength.

Share ways you have incorporated posturing in God's Word into your daily schedule. Did you have to give something up to make room? Did you need to rearrange your day?

ACTIVATION 2

b) Your heart is in the process of being healed by the Lord right now. And as He heals you, wounds are uncovered. Sometimes the wounds go so deep we have a hard time believing we will ever be fully healed. If you had difficulty reading any of the posturing verses above, there may be a wrong mindset or lie that is telling you you can't be healed. God loves to bring healing and restoration to your heart. Follow the steps below:

Choose one verse you find hard to accept. Which verse is it?

A wrong mindset or lie is revealed when we don't believe God for His Word. In this case, the lie may be that your experience was too bad, too extreme, and that you cannot be completely healed. Ask the Holy Spirit to show you what you believed in place of the truth. What did He show you?

Ask God to forgive you for agreeing with the lie and building a wrong mindset. Now verbally break the agreement you have had with the lie. Pray, "Lord, I'm sorry for believing a lie. It kept me from trusting You and believing Your Word. In Jesus' name, I break my agreement with that lie and command any demonic spirit attached to the lie to leave me now! I declare that the bondage is broken! I release the pain in my heart to You! I know You will help me with it. From now on, I believe _____."

Write the verse again in your own words.

Ask, "Lord, heal the specific place in my heart that was injured where the lie came in."

Sit quietly a moment. The Holy Spirit is healing you and soaking your heart in love. Now take a deep breath and read the verse again. Acknowledge that God is healing your heart.

ACTIVATION 3

c) Jesus came to heal the brokenhearted. (See Isaiah 61:1 and Luke 4:18.) Brokenhearted means crushed, shattered, and bruised. Close your eyes and ask the Holy Spirit to reveal the *next* place He wants to heal in your heart. Stay quiet and ask Him to soak your heart in His healing oil. Put your hand on your heart and say, "Heart, it's time to be healed." What did the Holy Spirit show you?

Go through the following steps:

1. Acknowledge the hurt.
2. Forgive whoever hurt you. Repent for any ways you contributed to the situation.
3. Tell any demonic spirits to leave.
4. Ask God to heal that hurt place.

What happened?

d) Read John 15:26 and Acts 9:31. What are some of the names of the Holy Spirit?

What did the Holy Spirit do for the people?

How does His comfort and encouragement enable you to fulfill what God has called you to do?

Based on both of the verses, what kind of friend is He to you?

Acknowledging and proclaiming the nature of the Holy Spirit is a powerful activation. The words coming out of your mouth hit the air around you and change the atmosphere! Once again, with your hand on your heart, close your eyes and say, "Holy Spirit, You are the great Comforter. I receive Your comfort. I receive Your encouragement."

Write about this activation.

e) Isaiah 53:3-5 is a prophetic picture of Jesus. From this passage we learn that He is familiar with our pain and grief and sorrow. Rewrite this passage in your own words.

Read Psalm 147:3. We have a precious promise from the Lord that He will heal our broken hearts. How have you seen God heal your heart in the past?

8. PRAYER: A HEALED HEART

a) Read the prayer. Add your own extra lines to this prayer.

a) What is God passionate about?

b) What are your thoughts and feelings about this Word?

notes...

COVERED IN RIGHTEOUSNESS

Delighting in Your Secure Position as a Blood-bought Child of God

Righteousness is a big word. What does it mean? Can we be righteous? What if we mess up? These are questions many Christians ask. The truth is righteousness is an amazing gift from God. Being the righteousness of God is our inheritance, and it's time to live and walk in the freedom that comes from being righteous before God!

I. READ ISAIAH 61:10 AND THE FIRST AND SECOND PARAGRAPHS OF CHAPTER 7 IN THE BOOK.

a) Isaiah compares our robe of righteousness to how a bridegroom adorns himself with ornaments and how a bride adorns herself with jewels. Think about how gloriously a bride can shine—the care she takes to look exquisite and special on her wedding day. Consider how handsomely and perfectly a bridegroom presents himself to his bride. Every detail is in place. The comparison is stunning! Now slowly and thoughtfully read the verse again. How does this comparison enhance your perspective on righteousness?

b) Define *righteousness.*

c) Many of us have a hard time believing we are fully accepted by God. We feel like we are failing God because we do not measure up. Have you ever felt this way before? Close your eyes and quietly ask the Holy Spirit to bring to mind a time when you were apprehensive that God was mad at you or that you didn't measure up.

d) For many, self worth is based on performance or perfectionism. In what ways have you found yourself succumbing to performance or perfectionism as a way to validate your self worth?

e) When God looks at you, He doesn't see what you used to be; He sees _____. You are clothed in His _____.

f) What does gaining a greater understanding of righteousness mean to you? Many believers struggle with comprehending that they are the righteousness of God in Christ. Have you had an eye-opening experience of seeing yourself covered in righteousness? Share.

a) A major ingredient of our true identity is

b) Righteousness destroys _____. It destroys feelings of _____. If you do something wrong, you are still _____. Believing you are righteous is _____ your identity. When we mess up, a slippery slope leads into an _____ trap in order to _____ right standing with God.

c) When we mess up, why do you think we tend to hide from God?

d) When we do mess up, what does the devil do?

e) When guilt and condemnation sweep in, we sometimes wrongly feel God's love for us has waned. Share a time when you began to believe that God loved you less because you made a mistake.

f) Sometimes we feel there is only one way to get right with God: we've got to

g) We then become embroiled in a lie. What lie?

a) Our righteousness—our right standing with God—has _____
to do with _____.

b) Righteousness was given to us because of

c) Read 2 Corinthians 5:21. "...so that in Him we might become the righteousness of God."
Take some time to let this verse sink in. What does this mean to you? How do you feel, knowing
that you now are the righteousness of God?

d) Jesus died in our place for our sins so that we could be _____ completely
_____ before God because we surrendered our lives to Jesus and
accepted Him!

e) Righteousness is a _____ from God. Once you are made righteous, the good things you do come out of _____ with Him. You have entered into a _____. What zone have you now entered?

4. READ THE LAST PARAGRAPH IN THE TEACHING SECTION.

a) Speaking the truth about your righteousness in Christ builds a

5. POSTURING: COMPLETELY COVERED IN RIGHTEOUSNESS.

Pray before you posture: "God, help me see the truth about what I am speaking. Breathe life on my proclamations and break off past thought patterns that are contrary to Your truth, in Jesus name." Declare all of the posturing verses out loud.

a) Which three verses stand out to you?

b) It takes discipline to diligently complete the Activation Manual and also posture in the verses daily. Describe how this journey of posturing has affected you.

ACTIVATION 1

a) People invariably hold on to secret mindsets of performance and perfection. Embracing righteousness shatters the lie of needing to perform to gain acceptance by God. Believing you are righteous destroys lies producing rejection and abandonment. You are in right standing with God. Jesus made sure of it. Condemnation cannot have you. Shame cannot beset you. Fear cannot overcome you. You know you have a covering from God called *righteousness*! This cloak is assaulted every day, and you must stand strong in your revelation of righteousness.

The price you pay to destroy wrong mindsets and replace them with heavenly mindsets is *time*. Sacrifice time this week to declare the verses from this chapter. Speak them over yourself first thing in the morning, as you're going through your day, and as you're getting ready for bed. Take every opportunity to proclaim these powerful words. Do this every day for at least one week. Remember to include posturing verses from the previous weeks as the Holy Spirit leads you. Even if you read only one additional topic a day, choose the one you need most. It is important to keep going over the previous posturing sections.

ACTIVATION 2

b) You are training yourself to recognize wrong mindsets. These lies or wrong mindsets that have crept into your beliefs are strongholds meant to keep you weak and powerless. When you believe a lie, you are not believing what God has established as truth—and this makes you weak. You will be hard pressed to operate in the supernatural ways of God when your mind is deceived. This is exactly why you are uncovering lies in every identity topic in this book. You are learning to identify and demolish lies. The position in your mind the lie had controlled is filled with the living Word of God. This is a life-long practice. I have equipped many to posture, and they are always amazed at how many lies they have unwittingly embraced. You will become more and more adept at discerning lies.

As you declared the verses, did you experience any resistance? Ask the Holy Spirit to show you one verse in the posturing section with which you felt resistance. What is the verse?

Somewhere along the way, you believed a lie. Lies create wrong mindsets. This lie (or wrong mindset) is hindering you from believing the truth. Quiet your heart and ask the Holy Spirit to help you identify the lie. What is the lie He helped you see?

Verbally break the agreement you have had with the lie. Say, "Lord, I am sorry for believing the lie. It has kept me from believing Your Word. In Jesus' name, I break my agreement with that lie, and I command any demonic spirit attached to the lie to leave me now! I proclaim this stronghold broken! Lord, heal the injured place in my heart where the lie came in. From now on, I believe _____."

Write the verse again in your own words.

ACTIVATION 3

c) Do you ever recall something out of your past that you are not particularly proud of? And do you hear a voice whispering in your ear, "After all you've done, God can't accept you. Don't fool yourself. You are unacceptable!" This accusation is so contrary to the truth. The devil doesn't play fair. He brings up old events from our past to sabotage us from believing that we have been made righteous. Once you accept His Son, God covers you completely with the righteousness of His Son. Close your eyes and think of an event from your past—one you know the devil tries to torment you about. Purposefully see the word *RIGHTEOUS* plastered over that event like a giant stamp from heaven. Say, "It is covered! I am righteous!" See yourself completely covered in robes of righteousness. What does knowing that the devil cannot torment you with your past mean to you personally?

d) According to Isaiah 61:10, we are covered in robes of righteousness. Let your creativity flow, and in the space below, draw a picture of what that might look like. What could be on the robe? Jewels? Colors? Feathers? Might music emanate from it? Light? Sound? Vibration? As you draw, tune into what the Holy Spirit is speaking to you.

To more fully complete the activation, we will do a prophetic act. A prophetic act is to interact with what is true in the spirit realm. Take this robe of righteousness you see with your spiritual eyes, and put on this stunning robe! Whether you sensed something or not, this prophetic act holds significance. What happened when you did this?

Activation 5

e) This last activation can be powerful. You are continually speaking words in your mind over your life. This activation directs you not only to speak over your life out loud but also to look in your eyes and make personal contact with yourself. Go to the mirror and, looking directly into your eyes, say to yourself: "You are covered in righteousness! The past is gone! You are the righteousness of God in Christ. When God looks at you, He sees the righteousness of His Son!" What is your inner response to this activation?

a) We can come to God with confidence, knowing that He accepts us. Add your own words to this prayer.

8. HEAVENLY WORD

a) What stands out to you the most in the Heavenly Word? Why does that truth affect you so strongly?

notes...

EXTRAVAGANTLY LOVED

Letting God's Love Embrace You and Fill You with Permanent Hope

We long to know God and of His love for us. But sometimes we wonder, "Does God really love me? Can I do anything to make God love me more? What if He's mad at me?" Scripture tells us that His love is everlasting, that it never fails, and that nothing can separate us from His love. It's time for us to know this unfailing love in the core of who we are. It's time to fully embrace just how *much* He truly loves us!

1. READ ROMANS 5:5 AND THE DEFINITION OF LOVE AT THE BEGINNING OF CHAPTER 8 IN THE BOOK.

a) This definition of love is amazing! Let's go over it in more detail.

Love: an undefeatable benevolence and _____ that always seeks the _____ for the other person, no matter what he does. It is the self-giving love that _____ without asking anything in return, and does not consider the worth of its object... the _____ God has for us.

b) God's love for us is radically unconditional. Undefeatable. Unconquerable. Now that is encouraging! What specifically does that mean to you?

a) Why does everyone have an innate desire to be loved?

b) What does your spirit cry out for?

c) Some of us were introduced to love through very loving mothers and fathers. Some of us began life with a very distorted view of love. According to the second paragraph, you have been craving to know that you are _____, that you are the _____, that you are loved for _____ not for _____, that if you screw things up you will still not be abandoned.

d) Maybe you are just beginning to experience God's love. Maybe you've experienced some off-the-charts love encounters with God. Share about how you experience God's love for you.

e) Worldly love always has conditions, but God's love is different; you can't _____ to deserve it.

f) As our Heavenly Father, God is far different from our earthly parents. As we get to know God the Father, most of us start off by relating to Him as we did to our own earthly fathers and mothers. When you were growing up, what was your love relationship like with your father? Or with the person who held this role in your life? You don't need to dig deep. Just state your initial feelings.

g) What was your love relationship like with your mother? Or with the person who held this role in your life.

3. READ PARAGRAPHS FOUR THROUGH SEVEN.

a) God's love for you is _____. He loves you the _____ whether you have a big Billy Graham Crusade ministry or a hidden, unknown, be-kind-to-your-neighbor ministry.

b) Have you ever thought, "If only I prayed more, if only I evangelized more, if only I was more like so-and-so—I would then be more acceptable to God, and He would love me more." What thoughts like this come to you?

Now shake those feelings off and approach God with a clean mindset, knowing that you are loved just as you are!

c) Read 1 John 4:8b. God does more than just love us: God *is* love. God will love you on and on and on and on—through all of your trials, your victories, your boring, quiet times, your failures—everything. How does this affect how you see God?

d) Read 1 John 4:19. If you feel you have only a small measure of love for God, remember that our love for Him originates with Him. We love Him because

e) The greatest demonstration of God's love for us was His sacrifice on the cross. It was the day Jesus said to His Father, "not My will, but Your will be done" (Luke 22:42). Essentially He was saying, no matter the pain, no matter the cost, he is worth it, she is worth it—YOU are worth it! Take some time to think about Jesus' death. Think about what He endured. It was all for you. You can write your thoughts in the space below.

4. Read the last three paragraphs of the first section of the chapter and answer the following question.

a) We put up walls to protect ourselves. All of us do it. Walls aren't always bad. At times they are boundaries that are very much needed. With God, it's different. He does not want anything to stand in the way of our love relationship with Him. As we grow in our understanding of God, life-long walls of protection and separation start coming down. Some of us have kept God out of certain areas of our lives. Take a moment to think about this: What are some of the areas to which you've not allowed God access? For you to more fully embrace your love relationship with God, invite Him into your *entire* heart. Are you willing to take a step of faith? Write out a prayer inviting Him in.

5. POSTURING: Embracing God's Love

a) Which three verses do you enjoy posturing in the most?

ACTIVATION 1

a) The most effective and immediately life-changing aspect of *The Real You* is speaking God's Word. You can answer all the questions and fill in all the blanks, but *posturing* is where you actively cooperate with the supernatural transformation of your mind. Be diligent. Be a warrior. Be dangerous. The Word in your mouth makes you dangerous. Every day this week, soak in these verses. To really solidify them into your mind and heart, proclaim them at least twice a day—once in the morning and once at night before bed. The morning prepares you for the day. Posturing at night prepares you for dreams and visions during the night. Posture yourself to be more aware of times you sense God's love pouring out on you. Remember: "For the Word of God is *living* and *active*" (Hebrews 4:12a). The posturing verses do not come from the world or the wisdom of man. They are directly from God, and God's Word is alive and life-changing!

How is posturing in love affecting you this week? What kind of inner change has taken place for you to receive more of God's love?

ACTIVATION 2

b) Being loved by God is so fulfilling. His love covers us like a thick blanket. When we know we are loved by Him, we can do anything. But sometimes, we have a hard time believing that He loves us. If you had a difficult time speaking any of the verses, you may believe a lie about God's love.

Look over the posturing section and see where your heart did not fully engage with a verse. Which verse did you have a hard time believing?

When we do not accept the truth, we align ourselves with a lie—whether bold or subtle. The devil is a trickster. A lie may sound good and feel good, but it is a deception. Through deceptions, strongholds are constructed. Now, ask God to show you the lie that has kept you from fully believing this truth about God's love. What is it?

Then quiet your heart and ask God to forgive you for believing the lie. Verbally break the agreement you have had with the lie. Say, "Lord, I am sorry for believing the lie. It has kept me from believing Your Word. In Jesus' name, I break my agreement with that lie and command any demonic spirit attached to the lie to leave me now! The bondage is broken! From now on, I believe _____." Write the verse again in your own words.

Now take a few minutes to let God heal the place in your heart that believed that lie. Ask Him, "Lord, heal the injured place in my heart where the lie came in." If He shows you anything about this wound, write it down and let Him speak life and truth to your heart.

ACTIVATION 3

c) Activations further *activate* each truth more fully in your life. This activation can be powerful, so don't skip over it. Using the Bible as your guide, write a love letter from God to you. Based on Scripture, what does God say to you about His love for you?

Dear Beloved One,

Love, Your Heavenly Father

ACTIVATION 4

d) Think of some of the love songs you have heard over the years. Ask the Holy Spirit to help you choose a love song and make it your song with God. Have fun! Change around the words. Here's an example: I love an oldies song that says, "Stay just a little bit longer! Oh, won't you sta-a-ay just a little bit longer!" Only, my heart sings it, "Holy Spirit, stay just a little bit longer…!"

What song did you choose? Write the lyrics on the lines below with your own changes.

e) Set an atmosphere of love and spend quiet time with God. Light candles, play worshipful music, and do whatever sets an intimate atmosphere for you. Read Psalm 63:1-3.

What does this Psalm say of God's love and seeking God?

Close your eyes and draw close to God. Consider how He has changed your life. Think about the encounters you have had with Him. Now write *your* love letter to Him.

Dear Precious Lord,

Love,

7. PRAYER: EVER INCREASING LOVE

a) Add a few lines of your own to the prayer.

8. HEAVENLY WORD

a) Watch for Him throughout your day. Journal how you recently felt His kisses from heaven. It could be through a song, a Scripture, a time when you felt Him near—any way that you felt His love showering you this week!

notes...

POWER AND AUTHORITY

Administrating God's Delegated Power and Authority on the Earth

Jesus said that all authority has been given to us. What does this authority look like? How do we use this authority to shift our lives and shift our atmospheres? Let's take a look.

I. REFER TO PARAGRAPHS ONE AND TWO IN CHAPTER 9 OF THE BOOK.

a) "From that day forth, I inherited a whole new realm of authority." Have you ever thought of marriage as imparting authority? Can you give some examples of how a wife has an expansion of authority and privileges once she is married?

b) Who else operates in authority? Share some examples of people who have been given authority. (Example: a policeman)

a) God _____ us up with Christ and _____ us with Him in the heavenly realms. Being seated with Jesus at the right hand of the Father carries tremendous _____ and _____ for us. Jesus is seated far above all _____ and _____, and all things are under His feet—all things!

What does this pertain to?

b) Since Jesus is the head and we are His body, we hold this position of

c) What does knowing you have authority over the demonic realm mean to you?

d) Why do you think your authority as a believer in Christ is severely tested?

e) Read Isaiah 61:1-3. Jesus told us that we would do all He did and more. What were some main ministries of Jesus that were passed on to you?

There are three steps listed in this paragraph that will help us fully grasp the authority delegated to us.

a) First, _____ has been given to Jesus.

Which verse declares this truth?

b) Next, Jesus _____ His authority to _____.

What scripture supports this truth?

c) What two words are interchangeable?

d) Furthermore, Jesus directed us to pray that God's will would be done on earth as it is in heaven. Where in the Word do we see Jesus pray this?

e) How do we know His will?

f) We get a glimpse of God's will by looking at the works of His Son. Give some examples of Jesus' works.

4. LOOK AT PARAGRAPH NINE.

a) What is another aspect of operating in Jesus' authority?

b) Where have you seen the power of the name of Jesus in your own life?

a) Describe the posture David took in his life.

b) We are the ones who must choose to maintain an _____ posture so that God's will and purposes may be established on earth.

c) Your situation may not change as quickly as you would like. Do not get _____. You are on track. Some victories are instantaneous, but others require a full on war that must be won, one _____.

d) With the authority of Christ Jesus, we are able to _____ and _____ all the power of the enemy. The same anointing that was upon Jesus, empowering Him to destroy the works of the devil, is upon *you*! How does believing this truth affect your life?

e) Authority is in you _____. We all have the same amount of authority. The difference is in what you _____ about your authority and what you _____ with your authority.

6. POSTURING: Power and Authority

a) What are three of your favorite verses?

b) Why are these three verses your favorites?

7. IDENTITY ACTIVATIONS: Your Authority as a Believer

ACTIVATION 1

a) When you first begin speaking the truth about your authority, your mind may need time to adjust. Many people have an inner thought-life that is replete with limitations and dead ends. Posturing in your true authority will compel the truth of your authority in Christ to go deep down into your heart where you will really believe it. And then you will find yourself acting on it in your daily life. It's a game changer!

Each time you take a stance (posture) in the truth of God's Word, you weaken a stronghold of passivity and build confidence in your authority. Passivity wants us to ignore the spiritual war, to lay aside our sword and forget about our authority. Passivity is grounded in unbelief. We need to learn how to fight battles and not run from our calling and authority. Feel the stirring deep down inside rising up in you. Listen to the still, small voice reminding you of who you are in Christ, encouraging you to yield your life to Him. Just as you have received Jesus, so walk in Him. Envision the greatness God has placed in you, and step into the center of the ring. He has equipped you to stand against the schemes of the enemy and take hold of all your inheritance in Christ Jesus. Come on! If you want it, you are well able to obtain it!

You may have substantially functioned in authority already. Now we want to blast authority open by aggressively speaking and soaking in authority—more than ever before. Speak all the authority verses twice a day. Remember, posturing is the core of this study. If you do nothing else—speak these verses. Review the verses of past weeks as well. You are on the home stretch!

Thoughts?

ACTIVATION 2

b) Follow the steps below:

Find one verse you are having difficulty believing, and write it here.

Ask the Holy Spirit to show you the wrong mindset you have held that hindered you from believing the truth of this verse. What is it?

A wrong mindset is a lie. Ask God to forgive you for believing the lie. Verbally break the agreement you have had with the lie. Say, "Lord, I am sorry for believing the lie of _____ _____. It has kept me from believing Your Word. In Jesus' name, I break my agreement with that lie and command any demonic spirit attached to the lie to leave me now! I proclaim that the bondage is broken! From now on, I believe _____."

Write the verse again in your own words

Ask God to heal your heart where the lie came in. Relax. Soak in God's presence. Accept that His authority and power live in you right now. See it! Feel it! Close your eyes and feel power and authority in you—deep within.

ACTIVATION 3

c) Look at the posturing verses. Choose a favorite verse. With this activation, you will take the verse with you in study and prayer for deeper understanding. With each verse, there are unending layers of revelation. Ask God about the verse. Ask Him to open the eyes of your heart for more understanding. Ask Him for the Spirit of wisdom and revelation concerning the verse. Which verse did you choose?

Look up the verse in several translations, and write them. Also look up key words in the verse in a dictionary and write the definitions.

Paraphrase the verse in everyday language.

Write your paraphrased version of the verse in first person.

Did you receive additional revelation when you continued to pray and study the verse?

ACTIVATION 4

d) Read the verses in Chapter 1. Now, with this fresh posture of authority, approach these verses. Taking authority over wrong mindsets with newly gained knowledge of your authority will alter how you interact with these verses. How is speaking the verses on your thought-life different for you now?

ACTIVATION 5

e) You will gain greater understanding when you investigate two Greek words for power and authority: *Dunamis* (Strong's 1411) and *exousia* (Strong's 1849). Look these words up in reference books and online. How are these words used? What insights does this research give you about power and authority?

8. PRAYER: Your Authority In Christ

a) Share three areas where can exercise your God-given authority more.

9. HEAVENLY WORD

a) This is an exciting word from God! What part stirs your heart the most in this word?

notes...

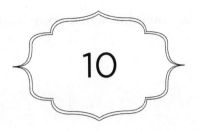

10

CREATED TO OVERCOME

Overcoming all the Works of the Enemy by Understanding Your Victory in Christ

Beloved, you have been created to overcome. An overcoming spirit flows through you and rests upon you. The seven letters to the seven churches in Revelation speak of the rewards you receive because you are an overcomer! You do not carry an "I can't" in your spirit. You carry an "I can overcome!" in your spirit! God's Word is full of promises that declare your position of victory. It's time to step into the full revelation of this truth!

1. READ PARAGRAPHS ONE AND TWO IN CHAPTER 10 OF THE BOOK.

a) Look at the definition of *overcome*. What pictures, thoughts, or people come to mind when you think of the word *overcome*?

b) Life is all about perspective. According to the chapter, from which vantage point do *insurmountable hurdles* look vastly different?

Can you give an example from your own life when your attitude about a situation changed as you saw it from God's perspective?

c) Give an example of how you would *fight from victory*.

d) You are _____ with _____ you need to overcome.

e) 1 John 5:5 states, "Who is it that overcomes the world? Only he who believes that Jesus is the Son of God." Our part is to _____ the posture of an overcomer and _____ God.

2. READ PARAGRAPHS TWO, THREE, AND FOUR.

a) Gideon saw himself from a weak, defeated perspective. God, however, saw him in his _____. He saw him as a _____. So it is with you. God sees you _____ not in linear time.

b) God sees you in the fullness of your future. He sees you as a warrior and overcomer. Based on all you have studied so far in *The Real You*, how else does He see you?

c) The future is in you _____. God has
_____ it. The DNA of a _____ has already
been downloaded into you.

d) Where are our strength and courage centered?

In the _____. He goes before us as a mighty
breaker—breaking open the way for _____.

e) Every day you have the opportunity to apprehend another promise. These promises can also
be called your Promised Land or territories. What promises has God spoken over your life?

f) Each time you overcome opposition, your opposition _____
and no longer has jurisdiction over you. That which you _____ you
_____.

g) Can you think of a time when you overcame something and you then had power and
authority over it when you faced it again?

3. Look at paragraph five.

a) Words are powerful — powerful enough to overcome. How does this change your perspective on the power of your words?

4. POSTURING: Positioned as an Overcomer

a) Which three verses strengthen you the most?

5. IDENTITY ACTIVATIONS: Activating the Overcomer in You

ACTIVATION 1

a) Declaring yourself an overcomer is powerful. The devil does not want you to think like this. He comes to steal your true identity and destroy it. You have to fight for it. You have to be like Jesus and say, "It is written!" Recognize that there is a war going on! You have to fight to change your mindsets to posture yourself as an overcomer. Trials and difficulties will come. So you must *believe* this vital truth about your identity! You must conquer this land! I speak to you as a mother in the faith. Do not wonder if you are going to make it—if you can overcome. *Know* and *believe* you have been endued with power from God to overcome! Because it can take time to rewire your mindsets and believe you are an overcomer, this activation is imperative. Speak these verses twice a day. This day you fight!

b) Trials are difficult. At times, we don't think we will get through them. We cannot see an end in sight. This is exactly why it is vital that we see ourselves as overcomers. If you find you have fallen out of your posture as an overcomer—simply reposition yourself. Do not condemn yourself—reposition yourself. Remember—you are transforming.

What verse do you have a hard time fully believing?

What is the lie hindering you from believing the truth of this verse?

Now quiet your heart and ask God to forgive you for believing the lie. Verbally break the agreement you have had with the lie. Say, "Lord, I am sorry for believing the lie. It has kept me from believing Your Word. In Jesus' name, I break my agreement with that lie and command any demonic spirit attached to the lie to leave me now! I declare the bondage is broken! Lord, heal the injured place in my heart from where the lie entered. From now on, I believe _____."

Write the verse again in your own words.

c) The next activation is a concept I gleaned from worship leader Jake Hamilton. Meditate on the opening verse for this chapter, 1 John 5:5. If you take your time with this, you will begin to imbed the revelation of this verse in your heart. It can take time for a verse to move from your head down to your heart. So take your time and enjoy the process. God loves spending time with you. And He really wants to take you way below the surface of the words on a page.

Begin by writing the verse at the top of a blank page. Slowly speak it out loud and ponder every word. Think of yourself as doing this with God.

Next, write it out creatively. Draw pictures, doodle, and interact with it. Try speaking the verse over and over, emphasizing different words.

Explore singing it. Spend time singing it, whether you think you can sing or not. God likes you, and He likes you singing His Word. Get creative. Even dance! I'll give you an example. A few months ago I was spending time with God and the song "Let It Rain" came on my iPod. I danced all over the room like Gene Kelly in *Singing in the Rain!* I could feel the pleasure of the Lord.

Finally, pray it. Really explore the verse in prayer. Take off with the verse in your own words.

Describe how this process unfolded for you.

ACTIVATION 4

d) What obstacle are you facing? Ask the Holy Spirit to help you complete the following sentence: "In my life right now, in order for me to move forward, I must overcome…"

Ask the Holy Spirit to show you your next steps for overcoming this obstacle. Write down the steps the Holy Spirit showed you in overcoming this hurdle. Develop an action plan for how and when you will take the first step.

ACTIVATION 5

e) God is calling you just like He called Gideon. You may be hiding in the middle of your own winepress. But God is calling you a mighty man or woman of valor. Ask the Holy Spirit to show you what you look like as an overcomer. Take the image He impresses on you and draw it. Draw your own wildly creative picture of you as an overcomer. This is a prophetic act. You are activating the overcomer in you with a visual.

6. PRAYER: Being an Overcomer

a) Write out this prayer and post it in a place where you will see it every day—like your bathroom mirror, your dashboard, or above the toilet paper.

7. HEAVENLY WORD

a) Living from your true identity means living from a heavenly perspective, where Christ is seated above all powers and authorities. You are sitting with Him there right now. Look up Ephesians 1:20-23 and journal your insights on the chapter.

notes...

A Personal Message from Linda Breitman

Congratulations! You have completed a very high-level identity training! I know the Activation Manual challenged you. As a spiritual mother in the faith, I am proud of you!

Posturing week after week builds character in you. You can pray and read the Word of God, but the way character is built is by the *choices* you make as a result of all you have learned. You have chosen to be diligent and to persevere. The decisions we make that truly build our character are not always easy. The path is narrow. Building godly character takes time. Finishing this manual demonstrates that you have tapped into a persevering spirit. Good job!

I encourage you to continue posturing in all of the verses in this book. Consider what God said to Joshua. In Joshua 1:8 the Lord said, "Do not let this Book of the Law depart from your mouth; meditate on it day and night, so that you may be careful to do everything written in it. Then you will be prosperous and successful." In other words, keep speaking what is written. Keep Scriptures coming out of your mouth. Doing so will compel you to think about what you are speaking. You speak the Word and meditate on it.

I have been working on a sequel to *The Real You*. The focus will be on functioning at a more advanced level of your identity from which you engage and partner with the Holy Spirit. The training will include topics like getting pictures from God, dreaming with God, engaging with the Holy Spirit, and developing deeper intimacy with God. Check in with me at www.LindaBreitman.com for a sneak peek.

In the meantime, let us know how *The Real You* impacted your life. I would love to hear from you. I am passionate about building identity and releasing destiny. Email our office though our website.

Blessings to the real you,

Linda Breitman

ANSWERS

CHAPTER 1: ALIGN YOUR THOUGHTS WITH HEAVEN

1a. What is true, noble, right, pure, lovely, admirable, excellent, and praiseworthy (NIV).
1b. Rejoice, do not be anxious, by prayer, petition, and thanksgiving present your requests to God. And His peace will guard your heart and mind.
1c. Your answer.
1d. Your answer.
2a. Your answer.
2b. Your answer.
2c. Your answer.
2d. When you align your mind with God's perception of you.
2e. War zone, battlefield, dominance.
2f. We feel encouraged.
2g. Your answer.
3a. "...the Holy Spirit begins leading us into a new world of thought—a world of thinking outrageous, supernatural God thoughts."
3b. We are transformed.
3c. We do. Wrong, negative, replace, true.
3d. Limited. Earthbound.
3e. Your answer.
3f. Your answer.
3g. Your answer.
3h. Demolished, destroyed, replaced.
4a. Daily.
4b. Do not. Refuse. Your answer.
4c. Purposefully, praying, declaring.
4d. By looking deeply at what Scripture says about how we think and what we think.
4e. Breaking agreements, confronting. Planting, building, establishing, Scripture.
5a-6g. Your answer.
7a. Heavenly realms.
7b. Your answer.
8a. The supernatural life with God.
8b. Death, life.

Chapter 2: Your New Identity

1a.	Your answer.
1b.	The adjustment of the moral and spiritual vision and thinking to the mind of God, which is designed to have a transforming effect upon the life.
1c.	Your answer.
2a.	Your answer.
2b.	Your answer.
2c.	Learn what God says about you and believe it.
3a.	Believe. Act. Speak. Your answer.
3b.	The identity of Jesus.
3c.	By proclaiming the truth and authority of the written Word.
3d.	Decreeing, Scripture, authority.
3e.	Your answer.
4a.	Stunningly courageous. Wildly loved. Gifts, abilities, activate. Hope, future. Your answer.
4b.	Your answer.
4c.	Identify them, make a determined switch, and replace them with truth.
5a–8a.	Your answers.

Chapter 3: Transformed into His Likeness

1a.	To undergo a complete change which, under the power of God, will find expression in character and conduct.
1b.	Into His likeness.
1c.	Metamorphosis, change.
1d.	His face shone like the sun, and his clothes became as white as the light.
1e.	Your answer.
1f.	Love, character. Countenance.
1g.	Romans 12:2, 2 Corinthians 3:18, Matthew 17:2. In Romans 12:2 and 2 Corinthians 3:18 – transformed, Matthew 17:2 – transfigured.
2a.	Courage and obedience. He continually asked the Lord for direction.
2b.	He was humble, transparent, strong, and decisive.
2c.	Perseverance. Joseph persevered through many trials.
2d.	She was fearless.
2e.	He entered into the presence of God like a child, worshiping in complete freedom.
2f.	She was a warrior and very discerning about how to enter into battle.
2g.	He walked in authority. People were healed by his shadow.
2h.	Your answer.
2i.	Your answer.
3a.	Greater works that even He does.
4a.	The eternal now is outside of time. God sees you from the eternal now. Your true identity is in full bloom in the eternal now. When you posture, you are tapping into the eternal now.
4b.	Divine.

4c.   Grow.

4d.   Reality, transformation, call forth.

4e.   Godly attributes.

5a.-7a.   Your answer.

8a.   We shall be like Him.

CHAPTER 4: TOTALLY ACCEPTED AND HIGHLY VALUED

1a.   Your answer.

1b.   Worth much, precious, highly esteemed.

2a.   Your answer.

2b.   Your answer.

2c.   Your answer.

2d.   Your answer.

2e.   Our individual self-worth.

2f.   Love, accept.

2g.   Your answer.

2h.   Believing God loves us and accepts us.

2i.   Believing. True value, self worth.

3a.   Your answer.

3b.   We end up either not feeling good about ourselves, or getting puffed up with pride because we think we are so great.

3c.   Performance, God's eyes.

4a.   Your answer.

4b.   You were planned, You were wanted.

4c.   God the Father. Value, everything. You.

5a.   You were created with a unique personality, and you have unique gifts. You hold a position in the body of Christ only you can hold. No one is like you. Without you, there is a gap, a hole. Whether or not you realize it, your life is significant. You have been called and chosen to live a meaningful life that has great impact on the people around you.

5b.   The worth of that purchase.

5c.   The Blood of His Son.

5d.   We are worth everything to Him.

6a.   Opposing voices are destroyed and the foundation of God is built up.

7a.-10a.   Your answer.

CHAPTER 5: COMPLETELY FORGIVEN

1a.   Your answer.

1b.   Your answer.

1c.   Your answer.

2a.   Forgives us for it all.

2b.	Telling God you're sorry and then turning your back on the sin. Repentance is a 180-degree turnaround. It's a change of mind, resulting in a change of action.
2c.	Your answer.
2d.	Take revenge, hurt back, we don't like them. Ourselves.
2e.	Binds us with chains, keeps us from entering into. Us, true identity.
2f.	Truly follow in the footsteps of Jesus.
2g.	Your answer.
2h.	God. Big picture. Job.
2i.	Your answer.
3a.	God will not forgive us.
3b.	Your answer.
3c.	Inner torment. Peace. Victory. Freedom.
3d.	Climb down out of the judge's seat, forgive. His strength.
3e.	No.
3f.	Faces the wrongdoing, calls it wrongdoing, and then rises above it, releasing the ongoing damage and pain caused by that wrongdoing. Forgiveness is a choice to trust God to be your Defender and Final Judge.
3g.	No. We do. Bondage.
4a.	Self-condemnation, self-loathing.
4b.	Forgive and release yourself. Your answer.
4c.	Your answer.
4d.	Your answer.
4e.	Your answer.
5a–8a.	Your answer.

CHAPTER 6: A HEALED AND RESTORED HEART

1a.	To repair and restore to its original, perfect condition.
1b.	Admitting the pain.
1c.	Your answer.
2a.	Healed. Your answer.
2b.	Releasing you from all oppression and healing your heart.
2c.	Major wounds, hindered. Your answer.
3a.	Repentance. Forgiveness. Faith. Negative words spoken over a person's life.
3b.	Letting go of the past. Identity. Trap. moving forward. Heal the broken hearted.
3c.	Your answer.
4a.	Hurt, anger.
4b.	Anger tries to cover up the hurt so we don't feel it so deeply. Anger is wicked. It can consume a person, bringing sickness to the body and separation from people.
4c.	Your answer.
5a.	Somebody wronged you. First step.
5b.	Speaking. Unfolding process.
5c.	Tormenting spirit. You can tell the spirit of fear to leave in Jesus' name. Demonic spirits.

5d.   Ask God to heal your heart, believe Him for your healing. Thank Him for your healing.

6a. -8a. Your answer.

9a.   Seeing your heart whole and healed—and full of joy!

9b.   Your answer.

CHAPTER 7: COVERED IN RIGHTEOUSNESS

1a.   Your answer. Example: God's robe of righteousness that covers me is so very beautiful. It is vibrant with life and color!

1b.   Just, right standing, right relationship with God.

1c.   Your answer.

1d.   Your answer.

1e.   Jesus, robes of righteousness.

1f.   Your answer.

2a.   Righteousness.

2b.   Rejection. Inferiority. Righteous. Believing. I-need-to-do-works-and-perform, reinstate.

2c.   Because the shame is so great.

2d.   Turns a spotlight on our sin.

2e.   Your answer.

2f.   Do better, be better.

2g.   The lie of having to do works to be acceptable by God.

3a.   Nothing, our performance.

3b.   Our faith in Christ.

3c.   Your answer.

3d.   Declared righteous, justified.

3e.   Gift. Relationship. Partnership. Miracles, signs and wonders.

4a.   Righteousness consciousness.

5a-8a. Your answer.

CHAPTER 8: EXTRAVAGANTLY LOVED

1a.   Unconquerable goodwill, highest good, gives freely, unconditional love.

1b.   Your answer.

2a.   We were created that way by a loving Father.

2b.   His affirmation, to know you are valuable, special, and unique.

2c.   Accepted, favorite, who you are, what you do.

2d.   Your answer.

2e.   Do anything.

2f.   Your answer.

2g.   Your answer.

3a.   Unchanging. Same.

3b.	Your answer.
3c.	Your answer.
3d.	He first loved us.
3e.	Your answer.
4a–8a.	Your answer.

CHAPTER 9: POWER AND AUTHORITY

1a.	Your answer.
1b.	Your answer.
2a.	Raised, seated; power, authority, principality, power; everything in the demonic realm.
2b.	Authority and power over the demonic realm.
2c.	Your answer.
2d.	Your answer.
2e.	Your answer.
3a.	All authority. Matt. 28:18.
3b.	Delegated, us. Luke 10:19.
3c.	Authority and power.
3d.	Matt. 6:10.
3e.	We read His book, study how the apostles had authority, and how Jesus demonstrated authority.
3f.	Your answer.
4a.	The power of the name of Jesus.
4b.	Your answer.
5a.	Your answer.
5b.	Aggressive.
5c.	Discouraged. Battle at a time.
5d.	Defy, overcome; your answer.
5e.	Right now; believe, do.
6a–9a.	Your answer.

CHAPTER 10: CREATED TO OVERCOME

1a.	Your answer.
1b.	A heavenly realm vantage point. Your answer.
1c.	Your answer.
1d.	Fully equipped, everything.
1e.	Choose, believe.
2a.	Future. Mighty warrior. In your future.
2b.	Your answer.
2c.	Right now. Decreed. Champion.
2d.	Abiding presence of Jesus. Us to overcome opposition.
2e.	Your answer.

2f.   Loses its power. Overcome, own.
2g.   Your answer.
3a.   Your answer.
4a.–7a. Your answer.

ABOUT LINDA

Linda Breitman—spiritual mother, mentor, and author of *Going Fishing: Practical Ways to Reach Your Neighbor*, is an ordained minister and international conference speaker. She has been a featured guest on the 700 Club and numerous radio and television programs. Linda grew up in San Jose and has lived all over the Northwestern United States. She and her husband settled in San Diego County in 1998. Since then, Linda has developed an intensified mentoring program with graduates who have moved on to become successful parents, business owners, ministry leaders, and missionaries. Linda currently holds Prophetic Intercession Training Schools, Dangerous Women Activation Seminars, and The Real You Identity Courses. She is passionate to see men and women rise up in their God given identities, becoming fully equipped to impact nations with a renewed mind and a supernatural lifestyle.

For more information about Linda Breitman, visit: www.lindabreitman.com

Lets Connect...

Facebook:
http://www.Facebook.com/Linda.Breitman

Twitter: @LindaBreitman
http://www.Twitter.com/LindaBreitman

THE REAL YOU
BELIEVING YOUR TRUE IDENTITY
CURRICULUM

Know what God says about you, believe in what He says, and activate it!

Featuring Seven Powerful Components:

- *The Real You: Believing Your True Identity*

- *The Real You Activation Manual*

- *The Real You Video Sessions*

- *The Real You Identity Decrees*

- *The Real You Identity Decrees CD*

- *The Real You Video Sessions for Leaders*

- *Soaking in Your True Identity CD*

These items can be purchased at:

LindaBreitman.com

notes...

CPSIA information can be obtained
at www.ICGtesting.com
Printed in the USA
BVHW02s0016261117
501238BV00015B/167/P

9 780989 411318